# Fall of the Last Petal

Dr. Ratikanta Mishra

BLACK EAGLE BOOKS
Dublin, USA | Bhubaneswar, India

Black Eagle Books
USA address:
7464 Wisdom Lane
Dublin, OH 43016

India address:
E/312, Trident Galaxy, Kalinga Nagar,
Bhubaneswar-751003, Odisha, India

E-mail: info@blackeaglebooks.org
Website: www.blackeaglebooks.org

First International Edition Published by
Black Eagle Books, 2025

**FALL OF THE LAST PETAL**
by **Dr. Ratikanta Mishra**

Copyright © Dr. Ratikanta Mishra

All rights reserved. No part of this publication may be reproduced, stored in a retrieval system, or transmitted, in any form or by any means, electronic, mechanical, photocopying, recording or otherwise without the prior permission of the publisher.

Cover & Interior Design: Ezy's Publication

ISBN- 978-1-64560-685-7 (Paperback)

Printed in the United States of America

*Poetry is the art of uniting pleasure with truth, by calling imagination to the help of reason.*
**Dr. Johnson**

*Poetry should try to give a 'criticism' of life.*
**Mathew Arnold**

*Poetry is feeling, confessing itself to itself in moments of solitude.*
**John Stuart Mill**
'What is Poetry ?' (1833)

*Poetry is the supreme form of emotive language.*
**I.A. Richards**
(Principle of Literary Criticism), 1924

*Language itself is poetry in the essential sense.*
**Martin Heidegger**

The poet's gift is the gift of perpetual discovery.
**Andre Gide**
(Fruits of the Earth)

*Poetry is nearer to vital truth than history.*
**Plato**
(What is Poetry?)

"*To see a world in a grain of sand*
*And heaven in a wild flower,*
*Hold infinity in the palm of your hand*
*And eternity in an hour*".
**William Blake**

I dedicate this humble endeavour to Lord Jagannath to bless the time of Ours in its Creative Evolution.

My parents who have made me learn the alphabet of life.

My father-in-law and mother-in-law have made me feel as one amongst them.

My elder brother and sister are the sources of inspiration in weaving this garland.

All my co-brothers deserve my adoration.

My spouse Usha and son Ronit have all along provoked me to go on a journey of self-discovery.

My younger brother Srikant has always been a companion and friend in my creative journey.

My litter sister 'Lakshmi' is exhilarated to see her elder brother writing poems.

During this period, I have had the rare honor and fortune to meet five friends and mentors who have finetuned my little potentials and inspired me to sketch the outlines of a poetic sculpture. They are Prof. Bibhu Padhi (Bibhu Bhaina), Prof. Fakir Mohan Sahoo, Prof. Prakash Chandra Mohapatra, Dr. Udaynath Majhi and Dr. Bhagaban Jaysingh. Names, I feel need no elaborate appendages.

I express my deep sense of gratitude to Sri Satya Patnaik, Founder of Black Eagle Publication, Ashok K. Parida, Country Head, Black Eagle Publication and Sri Pravat K. Mohapatra lovingly called 'Lipu' for their unstinted contribution in making my efforts see the light of the day.

AND<br>'YOU ALL'

My readers, critics the world over for your support and critical scrutiny.

Dr. Ratikanta Mishra

# Foreword

'Fall of the Last Petal' is my third collection of English Poems, the other two being 'Silence between two Words' and 'A Dialogue of Yesterday... Continues'.

A poet per se should not speak more. His poems should.

'Fall of the Last Petal' is an anecdotal metaphor of transformation of a beast into a man. To a pair of bare eyes, the fall of the last petal is the declaration of the death of the flower. A poet, however sees this whole episode to be a narrative of renewal and regeneration of life in the ever present Cycle of Life and Death. A petal returns to the womb and takes a rebirth to become a full-blown flower.

What we see is not the whole truth, a lot remains unseen. Life, the ever present knows no finality. Death also is not the end. To be prescient, there is no beginning and no end.

The Eliotesque narration in 'Burnt Norton' (No.1 of 'Four Quartets) is apt here to be quoted verbatim.

> "Time present and time past
> Are both perhaps present in time future
> And time future contained in time past".
> X X X
> "What might have been is an abstraction
> Remaining a perpetual possibility".

The poet does not have the sole and exclusive right over his poem. At times, poem chooses the poet. Words on their own dictate the poet to note down the lines. The only intellectual capital of the poet, if there is any, in his poetic sensibilities and perspective. Sensibility is his inward being and perspective is how he sees his surroundings. Sometimes the poet remains in the oblivion, outside the circumference of the poem. That is the discourse of his meditation, and salvation. What more does a poet need to prove his existence ?

My book is now in your hands for critical scrutiny which you have acquired with the language of your consciousness and wisdom. It gives me immense pleasure to expect my readers to have an open dialogue with the poems.

I am to conclude with the extract of the poem "Accomplice" by Jorge Luis Borges.

"They crucify me, I have to be the Cross, the nails.
They hand me the cup, I have to be the hemlock
They trick me, I have to be the lie
They burn me alive, I have to be the hell".
Need I say anything more after the extract ?

**Dr. Ratikanta Mishra**

# CONTENTS

| | |
|---|---|
| Thy Space I dare conquer | 11 |
| The Great Void | 15 |
| The Stanza remains incomplete | 18 |
| Losing the Identity | 20 |
| The Shadow of Infinity | 22 |
| The Innocent Shadow | 24 |
| Fractured Self | 26 |
| An Exile in My 'Self | 29 |
| An Evanescent Flame | 32 |
| The Metaphor of Surrealism | 35 |
| A Moment in Captured | 38 |
| Ethereal Sophistry | 40 |
| The Solicited Darkness | 43 |
| The Denial of Circumference | 46 |
| The Desolate Shore | 49 |
| ---- And beyond | 52 |
| The Ultimate Journey | 55 |
| Indeterminate Categories | 58 |
| The Golden Darkness | 61 |
| A paintbox of ashes | 64 |

| | |
|---|---|
| The Intimate Darkness | 66 |
| Blossoms into Eternity | 68 |
| Bare Ground | 71 |
| The Shriek of Silence | 74 |
| A Bend in the Equation | 77 |
| Sunrise in California | 80 |
| God Soliloquises | 82 |
| Multiple Horizons | 84 |
| The Butterfly flaps its wings | 87 |
| The Downward Branches | 90 |
| An Amiable Chaos | 92 |
| The Lonely Sailor | 95 |
| An Unfinished Sculpture | 97 |
| The Infidel Time | 99 |
| Immodest Shadow | 101 |
| Dust aswirl in Sunshine | 103 |
| The Cathartic Pause | 105 |
| Ashore comes the Oarsman | 108 |
| Fall of the Last Petal | 111 |

# Thy Space
# I dare conquer

'I'
The reclaimed space is
mine
I unfurl my flag of arrogance
there
The golden cage is
mine
Also the chains of liberty
and
the lock of freedom.

I love my conceits
rejecting the sweet lullaby
of a throne
I prefer to be a slave
forgoing the prologue of a
monarch
with a faint vision of
locating the slave
on the throne
for a fraction
of a second.

The king blinks at the
throne
The slave whispers to himself
in an unheard voice.

'II'
What then is
Yours ?
A palace with barbed fences
to separate
categorise
provoke the plebeians
into a stasis
not to question your Authority.

To put one
down the line
in a trance of
magical nihilism
to inhale incessantly
the fragrance of your
inverted awe
and
convoluted reverence.

'III'
From
not so a high podium
you weave the lyrics of
your deceitful adoration
almost sermon-like
only to anchor them all
to your safe bay.

I am on a path
created by a wise Architect
You're in a temple
Built by an Anonymous Sculptor.
I've seen Eternity
in the star-lit sky
You might
might not also
have seen a fragment of
Eternity
from the courtyard of your
Divine space.

By my side on the
path
with an evanescent moon
on the sky
as a mute witness
stands
an obstinate child
whispering to her nubile mother
'God is a person too
like you and me
in the futile search of a
Man
to go on a Pilgrimage with
Him
Whose end points He is
yet to trace and
locate.

**'IV'**
I conquer your space
Question me
I perish
Answer me
You're nowhere
in sight.

# The Great Void

A terrain
adjoining a plateau
encumbered by water
on all three sides
listens to not so clear
a voice
with its echoes
losing in the air.

The cadence of
the voice
with all
masculine virility
and
feminine grace
reveals a line
from ancient text.

The sky condescends
The earth evolves
The etherscape takes a shape
There lies the
epicentre of the Creation.

Atop the crevice
A monk and a
Prostitute
are to sow the
seeds of creation and
Destruction
in this Great Void.

This great void unfolds
itself
The lyrics of evolution
get a new
metaphor
to tell its own
narratives of
Being and
Nothing.

Tracing the lost
weird path of Being
the harlot moves
to a graveyard
of Immortal Sins
where
the horoscopes of Great Icons
are written and
erased
with no residues
at the end.

On the shrinking space of
Canvas
are deciphered

some syllables
evoking the motifs of
Idea without Idealism
Reason without Instinct
Progress without Morality
that are
fleetingly definitive.

The shadowy waves
from the embryo
of the Great Void
move
curlesque
with a vertiginous rapidity
to be born
reborn
in the womb of the etherscape
where the seaward monk
meets the horizon.

The Great Void remains
nonchalant in its fidelity
to Destiny
with a shimmering hope
for the arrival of
the monk and the
harlot.

# The Stanza remains incomplete

In front of a temple of
yore
a hopeful lesser mortal
begs for alms
fulfilment of desires
prays to move to that side of
lustful evening
and night of repentance
solicits divine presence to be
in the abyss of salvation
chants soulful rendition
in a mellifluous voice
lauding the charisma of
God
knowing little the
falsity of his prayer
and
truth of his pleasure
Seeks his compassion and grace
to be reimagined
reincarnated
from eternal to
ephemeral.
Explores the vacant space

between the line of the lore
locates the deep silences
between the two notes
only to find
in the end
that the stanza remains incomplete
and the syllables unuttered.

# Losing the Identity

The scar on the forehead of a
stranger
means a lot to me.

On a monosyllabic
note
I ask myself
Is he a misguided pilgrim
or
an insane lover
on whose forehead
life has had put
this touch of
anguish.

Heard a voice
afar
the pilgrim always loses the way
as
a lover meets the destined
insanity
in the end.

I'm yet to find my
space
in the grand puzzle of

Life.
Life has been very kind
to me
in pointing out a finger
at the graveyard
where the dichotomy of end and
beginning is resolved
and
I lose my identity
then and
there.

# The Shadow of Infinity

From a point here
to
the farthestmost tip of the
horizon
lies the empire of infinity
the ever expanding circumference of
Infinity.

I am
but
a speck of dust
on your pathways
to the Original Source of
Destination
Meditation
with a fledgling hope
and a
not yet fulfilled aspiration
I seek your
footsteps
on the journey
to partake of the
delightful anguish
that it entails
along the way.

During this sacred sojourn
I
touch the feet of all
Gods
Goddesses
Hermits
Prostitutes
and
untouchables alike
to get a profound heeling
that
the seeds of salvation lie in
a morsel of mud
and a
speck of dust.

From the mud
life blossoms
and into the debris
moves to take the
final shelter.

# The Innocent Shadow

Billowing tears
down the cheeks of a young girl
sow the seeds of
procreation of love
and
germination of life.

The butterfly
with a few teardrops
on its wings
whispers the petals
of the blossoming flower
reclining the mud wall
The girl is a flower
too
like you.
Rainbow overhead
blinks
at the girl and
the flower.

Evening descends
on the bosom of the Earth.
The mellifluous song on the lute
of the herd boy
permeates the fragrance of

love and despair
in equal measure.
The ray of the setting sun
illumines
both the pearls
and the carcasses.

The waves of the sea
erase
the footprints of
history and myth.

The young girl
moves in her
frozen dark path
to caress her own
shadow of disembodied shape
in sweet arrogance.

Little deaths
Fall from sky
like a shower of asteroids
to lie
in the palms of the girl
crumpled and
inert.

# Fractured Self

Selves of all hubris
merge in one
preaching the song of
beauty in Unity.

Thousand lamps are
lit
to celebrate the joyous spring
in our soul.

Death and despair
are
vanished,
lost in the
weird feminine darkness of
new moon.

The pot of nectar is
hung from the branches
of a peepul tree
by the sea side
achurned just a little while
ago
by the Gods and
demons alike.

Nearer the war field
a tired chariot is
reclined against a bar in regal robes
Dead bodies across the
battle line
talk
in an archaic language
of indeterminate intonation
never heard
in days of
yore.

The victor journeys towards the Deluge
The vanquished moves towards the throne
Armoury falls down to the ground
along the illusion of victory
and the reality of defeat.

The blazing torch
lits the funeral pyre
Masculine astral beams
are set afire
to sing the paeans of
Nothing
Nothing ever lives.

A few steps
up the attic
a grasshopper chants
the lore of Truth
'War was lost on that day
at that moment
in a court room of wise hermaphrodites

and arrogant fools
when
Draupadi was disrobed
dishonoured
to be the real 'Being
in a conglomerate
of neuter genders.

Up there
in the shady corner of the field
an asterisk of Destiny
with its rhythmic cadence
and crescendo
is visible to the Immortal.
The flute lies there
forlorn.

An ecstatic silence
ensues
hereafter.

# An Exile in My 'Self

Profound darkness eludes
me
The projected light of the center
lures me.

I now stand
at the crossroads of
a blind alley of hope
and
of desperation
an arch like gate of despair.

Intimate jealousy
I had sought for
to explore the delight of
relationship.

These days
envious light
engulfs me
like a neo-real object
to erase the
last vestiges of
infatuated mystery.

Like a refugee
in an occupied land
shorn of hatred and
armoury
I begged to leave the
door of security and
rationed food of the
vanquished state.

Unwittingly
the mellifluous vibrations in the air
from the ruined fortress
pushed me to the
forlon womb of a native wild forest
where on a tree top
you measure the longitude of
your half-clad aspiration
and the latitude of the real space.

A long recess of silence
ensues.
On a fine morning
after the sun rises in the East
the hungry ruler
from the crevice of a hillock nearby
declares with an exclamatory tone
punctuated with sublime fear
'The war is always between
Man and
Man.

One man ascends the Throne
to dehumanise the other

the other descends to the ground
to rejoice in his
perpetual serfdom.
Man
who do you choose
is always an
exile in himself and loses
a lifetime to segregate the
nectar from the poison.

The bugle of victory is
heard nowhere
Also the lute of desperation
The code of War
is yet to be decoded.

# An Evanescent Flame

Aeons pass
unnoticed
disguised
with all canons of serendipity
looking back
the footprints of an
anonymous traveller,
a morsel of food in a
silver pot
and the skeletal remains
of an age old whore
are seen
a few meters away.

Gazing into eternity
a beggar in
royal gesture,
stares in
gay abandon
at a lotus in the pond
with half mauled petals
and a broken stem.

An unwed mother
with tears and smile
on the face

retires to her hut
of mud walls and leaves
to be in a state of
geometric deliriurn
to say
in a Delphic voice
that the child in her womb
bears the identity of
his patriarchy.

Into the frozen state of
soft darkness
Night enters
surreptitiously
into the hut of the
girl
void
fills the space
with passing time
of eternal woes and
transient joy.

The lotus falls asleep
in the deep water of
pond.
The rainbow lurks
in the horizon.

The beggar
at regular
intervals
becomes a king
in his empire of

craft and
deceit.

The girls sees tomorrow
in the flickering flame
of hope and
hopelessness.

# The Metaphor of Surrealism

The myriad desires of
earth and heaven
come together
in parallel momentum
to conceal the conceit
of our nuanced existence
surreal as it is
though.

On the frontier of
time
charred flames of
agony and
spired anguish of
life
move in close proximity
to reach a
terrain of partial nihilism.

Emerging unscathed
the wise man
preaches the gospel of all
half-truths,
paints the image of
the contour lines of
white lies

Guileless truths are not to be
revealed
on the assumption of the
onset of a new
sunrise from the
East.
Truths subside
Half truths parade in the light of the day
with aplomb and assurance
of their long reign
on the dust and soil of
this Earth.

Lies
as white as lilies
blossom in the garden of
ours
to reveal the neo-reality
that paves the way
for life.

Bewildering attachment to earth
remains
craving for heavenly sensuality
lurking in the corner.

Reclining the lamp post
under the evening sky
a surrealistic figurine
waits
with bated breath
for the morning sun of
Tomorrow.

when the primal truth is
revealed
to the chagrin of
the priest.

# A Moment is Captured

The path of Time is
embellished with the
grace and beauty
of the moments
The influence and impact of Time is
at the same hour
distorted and reshaped by
the reality of moments.

Moments are not noticed everywhere
Nor
are they for everyone.
A minuscule of the cosmos
get soaked in the
shower of blessed moments.

There
on a narrow river isle
God
in an abandoned citadel
observes
the incessant march of Time
with punctuated momentum.
Time takes a pause
Time reflects upon itself
captures the abyss of life

the resurgence of death
the resilience in between
A whole new order
beckons
when the crown takes refuge
in a speck of dust
lying desolate like a broken toy
of a child.

Time surges ahead
invites
History
to set the narrative of the
wounded in the war
anonymous foot soldiers
who
otherwise are destined to be annihilated
from the pages of tomorrow.

To that cherished pedestal
moves this upward curve
calls all and sundry
who intermittently are at
the forefront of the war
of life
to join the celebration
where one sees all
in oneself.
That blessed moment is captured.

# Ethereal Sophistry

A pathway up above is
paved with wise echoes of the
Scriptures.
Mysteries to many
hoi polloi
known to a few
patricians
inheriting wisdom and light
from yesterdays
down the line.

Binaries of all hues
divide ours
in neat ways
I - He
We - They
Ours - Theirs
Priest - Devotee
Wise - Ignoble
The lines are drawn
The two streams flow in
opposite directions
source is lost somewhere.

On sacred occasions
the pot-bellied priests

chants hymns
quotes the scriptures
annotates between the lines
evocating the shadowy penumbra of
Ego.
I know which you don't
I know which you are not to know.

Reclining the adored trunk of Destiny
the man on the ground
with sanctimonious obeisance to the priest
bends down to the illogical dictates
of the priest.

The gullible devotee
obeys each and every
intonation of the worldly wise
incarnation of God.

He worships the priest
considering him to be a God-ordained
person
which he really isn't.
All his life
he remains a prisoner of the ethereal
sophistry of the priest
but
at the other end
he sucks the nectar of
love and light
defying all the canons of
syllogistic sophism.

The priest in a state of bondage
Is chained to the Iron pillar
The devotee in a state of liberty
Moves around the temple.

# The Solicited Darkness

Darkness is a
certitude
Axiomatically true
beyond the pale of doubt.
A gift of Nature
with a touch of
Divine sensibilities.

Layers of light from the
blue sky
descends
in regal repertoire
to add luminosity to the sands on the shore
opens up the petals of lotus in the pond
gives a feminine fragrance to the body
of the pubescent girl on the isle.

The reflection of light
pushes the chunk of darkness to the centre
of the circle
for a while
but fails to dispel the myth of
darkness.
Light only perpetuates the beauty of
darkness.

The first morning of the Universe
saw
the darkness coming out of the womb of the
Mother Earth
sucks the dew drops on the grass
permeates its existence in the leaves
and trunks of the trees
in the dark forest.

In the abyss of darkness
the sages meditates in the caves of deep
forest
the warrior scripts the charter of strategy
for the ultimate war
the sensuous lumpen meets the reclusive
harlot in the shanties of the city.
The child sleeps listening to the ghost stories
of his grandmother
the newly weds go to bed as a corporeal
commitment.

Light descends from the sky
of stars and galaxies
to make the equation of life
structured
prosaic
and self-revealing
with the twinkling of an eye
light relapses to its cosy space
and
darkness engulfs all of us
as a necessary corelate
in the Orwellian world of ours.

The intimacy with darkness
of ours remains
rooted
blossomed
as ever.

# The Denial of Circumference

Walls are built up
when
the dialogue between you and
me
is interrupted by the
calculus of power and
profit.

The whole begins to crumble
to pieces
under the anemic pressure of the units
The whole is no more an arch of
shade and security
units swirl around
hither and tither
in search of an
elusive individual identity.

Centrifugal
instincts
run amok
here, there
everywhere.

Times pass
Ideas move

Theorems change
The lines of limit get shifted
Now the time in ripe
to trace one's root
lineage
memories of yesterday
a desire to be connected
a requiem for lost infancy
a longing for paternal love
and solace.

With the narcissus like ego
at the acme of
near irrelevance
the chieftain of the tribe
ordered for the
falling down of walls
here
there
everywhere.

In the blizzard of uniting with
the centre
the tremors of Centripetal cyclonic
storm
decimated the walls of
yours
ours
and
mine also.

Lesser mortals felt a shock of
rejoice and

agony
The lines, at long last
of the circumference are
blurred
seen nowhere
Its existence is denied
in the long run
with the commandment of
the victory of Nature.

# The Desolate Shore

The fisherman in his cylindrical cap
and the loin cloth above his
knees
takes the boat into the deep sea
dancing to the tune of the sensual waves.

Here
on the shore
his wife and children
take adieu from him
with bated breath.

Far, far away
from the shore
and farther into the blue waters
all on a sudden
the fisherman became a stranger to himself
in his familiar sea and sky.

Cocooned and
aloof from
himself
in the quiet breeze blowing southwards
and the flimsy light of the
lantern
he met a sea angel

and narrated the
traumatic experiences
of his journey
from the shore to the
lap of the deep sea
and the undulating feelings
of tremor
of being alone and
aloof from the self
and
the same space he occupies
as others.

Days after
on his return from the blue sea
he encounters his shadow
under the star-spangled sky
to discover
much to his amusement and
bewilderment
that
he has not left the shore
yet
family stands as before
on the sands of the bank
The oars are
as a course
still tied to the boat.

The Oarsman comes ashore
is true
No less true is that
the seeds of morning lies
multilayered
in the womb of the evening.

# ....... And beyond

For aeons of time
not well-documented in recorded history
the scriptures of yore
with an aura of mystique
from mythology
tells the Day of Deluge.

The Universe is to be inundated
with the unflappable wings
of the waves of the blue sea
singing
the lyrical ballads of
Destruction.

The waves leave the shore
in search of the
steps of the crematorium and the
temple.
Afloat also the steps to
Heaven and
Hell
for escaping to a netherworld
of existential dilemma.

Here
here again

on this metaphysical space
man has to savour the
rare feelings of
heavenly curse and
hellish blessings.

One Universe
yes
only one is
in the grip of the Deluge.
But
millions of Universes
are lying there
unexplored
Can the little water of the sea
satiate the thirst of the
Universes?
Can the feeble waves submerge
the Universes?

Beyond the known
there's a crevice
a terrain
where Time and
Timelessness lose their
prologue
Images and shadows
betray each other
Reality and counter reality
elude one another
On the Throne
lies a chunk of sky
and a speck of earth.

The Epilogue of sea waves
meets its complete fragments
at the entrance of the mythical empire
and
a beyond follows
another
in its wake.
The postscript is yet to be
written
for posterity.

# The Ultimate Journey

The memories of Tomorrow
haunt me
The possibilities of Yesterday
scare me.

The 'I' in myself
seeks a space
with quotidian intent and
anxieties.

Shreds of existence
and
shards of its meaning
are scattered
here
there and
everywhere
on the shore and
beyond.

Along the shore
in the vast stretches of
casuarinas
the other 'self' of mine
lies
truncated

in the slits of the trees
descends
at times
to the nude lap
of the lady in
white saree
east wind turns puerile.

Am I then
to
inhale the stark fragrance of
the unconventional
nudity of
the lady ?

Am I to return
the lost shadow of
hers
lying in the tumultuous tides of the
sea ?

Am I to seek solace
in my corpse
wafting through the
frothy waves of the
sea ?

Am I to retrace
the prints of the anklets of
the widow
in the sand dunes of the sea shore ?

Am I to paint my image
in the diffused ashen fog
of the late evening ?

In the meadows of blooming flowers
of the night
I lie in the circle of
obscurity
to observe, inattentively
though
that the disrobed body of hers
and
my intimate corpse
move in
parallel lines,
pirouettes at times
like dancers
to the tune of the rhapsody of
life.

Am I then,
in the end
stand under the gaze of
evanescent moon light
to measure the depth of
Death
in absolute terms
bereft of reciprocity
and
relativity ?

# Indeterminate Categories

A needle-tip area of
land
expands and
merges with the Universe
loses identity
doesn't also
makes both the impositions
true and
false
in unequal measure.

At this moment
in a critical time like this
bereft of any meaningful discourse
a question
with existential contour lines
provokes all
to seek an answer
Definitive or
Otherwise
Does the shadow cast a spell
on the image ?

It does
however on a
vertical axis

with the upward growth of
wealth and riches.

After a long hiatus
of the Time frame
the expanded hinterland
contracts
mercifully
to a point within
to set the tone of a
horizontal elevation.

It is understandably
indeterminate
to say with some semblance
of certainty
that
elevation brings integrity
in its wake.

It's also
neither unmistakably
sure
in arithmetic terms
nor
clinically reliable
that
horizontal movement
in spatial terms
speaks
the prologue of
insightful inclusivity.

From the centre
to
circumference
man to
amoeba
all are relative
to one another.
Absolute
for any reason, though
is a misnomer.

# The Golden Darkness

In the primeval forest of Time
Someone, sometime
dares,
innocuously to
touch the petals of a
hibiscus flower
Time recedes
into the fold of mythology.

The shade of the tree
almost unerringly
provokes the 'He'
to pluck the fruit
and
eat a portion
with teeth mark on it
the residues for
all excepting 'He'
to partake the taste of
the forbidden fruit.

A little later
'She'
comes nearer to him
to decode him
with a lustful glance

to extend a Universe
beyond
this seemingly visible Universe.

The Throne
with all its profundity
descends and
finally acquires
the banality of
the space
that we inhabit
today.

We inhabit the Space and Time
where
darkness is mistakenly
proposed as light
when
wise men cunningly
preaches the futility of
this life
here and now
but,
ironically
lives in the cocoon of
amorous motifs.

The annals of history
revise the course of
Destiny.
The dropped anklets of the
court dancer
are disowned by the king.

Concedingly dismissive
Time
with its short memory and
blinkered vision
declares
the arrival of the Age of
Golden Darkness.

# A paintbox of ashes

Uncertain,
Unaware of the shape of tomorrow's wind
the density of the landscape of day after
tomorrow
the painter moves to
the deserted field
where
fourteen days ago
a disproportionate war of
Truth and
Evil
took place between
colossus of Hell
and
Pygmies of Heaven.

On the centre
in the middle of the
Path
the painter with two palmfuls of
History and
Mythology
draws his paintbox
only to find that
the tide of colors has
ebbed

on the shores of
Time.

Scratching the skin
of a corner
of the field
the painter
to his utter dismay
discovers
a potful of nectar
is placed
in the maize of an
urn of ash.

Bewilderingly gratified
the painter
added the nectar
to the ashes
and
paints a portrait
of his own image
with hands reaching out
to Hell
with an aspiration
to partake of
the sins of Heaven
when
the inward journey
comes to an end.

# The Intimate Darkness

On a moonlit night
in the blind alley of your civilised city
I'm in quest of immortal sins
and
mortal bliss
that are converged on
the jingle of anklets
and the abstract
silence of the danseuse
in an amphitheatre of the
banal aristocracy.

Radiating light
in an all encompassing
vortex of real darkness
coupled with ignorance
Her whirlwind movement of eyelids
and
spiralling 'mudra' in
amorous gesture
speaks eloquently
the post-truth, fake dignity
behind the façade of
proto-modernity.

The un(cultured) insects
in the dense dark night
smear all sins
on her body
and
comes out of the deep gorge
of
corporeal
pleasure on the next dawn of sunrise.


The worshipped angel of the
last night
keeps all agonies and suffering
close to her heart
with a soliloquy and
a prayer
for the ceaseless
churning of a
late twilight.

Staking my entire lifetime
what am I searching for?
But
a quadrangle of darkness
intimate and faithful
to the circle of Life.

# Blossoms into Eternity

On a summer day of
wild afternoon
a child in arms
while listening to the heartfelt
rendition of native lullaby
asks a question
with glows in his eyes
"will the butterfly not come to me
To be my friend"?

Eyes brimming with tears
heart broken
with a taunting fate
his loving mother
reclining a vast emptiness
prays for the fulfilment of
the wish of her child.

Inadvertently though
the child chases a
butterfly
and reached a garden
in heaven
richly embellished with
strange flora and fauna
surprisingly enough

the child felt within
himself
a vertical growth of
maturity
in asymmetrical
consonance
with Adam,
the Biblical man of aborigines.

Along the way
the angel came
sitting astride
a winged horse
to impress upon
the child
the language of half-revealed relationship
hinting at the other half
yet to be explored.

The mythical snake
behind the shrubs
of the desolate corner
arrived
hissing the sonorous lyre of
the other half-concealed relationship.

Now the moment of reckoning
beckons all
child, angel and snake
to blossom into
Eternity
Losing the tender touch of
Divinity.

The symbolic meaning of
Eternity
gets reflected,
radiated
in the firmly moored boats
on the shore
that can cross the sea-waves
in the tiny turmoil
knowing the depth of the
land
and the density of the ripples.

# Bare Ground

Standing on the bare ground
I dare touch the
torn feathers of the eagle
adrift on the waves
Dare I also
tear asunder
the beauty of the cosmic femininity
gleaming in the
obscene moonlight.
The temerity I have to
wake up the starving courtesan
anxiously waiting for
the benign gesture of the
royal gift.

With my feet firmly
on the ground
as a dispossessed
mute statue
I
In a self-interrogation
of sorts
depose
before you,
all strangers.

Have you ever noticed the teardrops in my eyelids
with any farthestmost signs of acquiring more and more?
Have your seen any change
in my behavioural
dynamics to luxuriate in royal glory?
Have I ever left the grey meadows of the grass
chasing the ivory linen bed of
regal embellishments?
Have I ever approached a wise harlot
leaning on the outskirt of the kingdom
to prepare a gameplan
to dethrone the monarch
and
take over the reins of authority
with correlates of
disproportionate arrogance?

The king is mired in
Self-doubt and
delusion to
draw a line between
image and
shadow
real darkness and
unreal light
truth diluted and
betrayal unalloyed
sitting on the throne
the king fears no one else
except his 'SELF'.

The king fears to touch the
bare ground
leaving the throne behind.

Grounded deep and
dense
I can only hope for an
undetermined happiness and
axiomatic suffering
only if I live till
tomorrow.

## The Shriek of Silence

In a grey silent world
wind from the east
and
the sunrise
whets up
an almost cosmic air of
expectation.

Hopes and aspirations are
belied
decimated
mingled with the ether.
Disillusionment grows with
apocalyptic exuberance.
Disenchantment pervades the air
With multi-hued abstraction
And
Multi-layered obscurity.

Days later
on a summer solstice
Quietly,
a dawn rises
the cast shell
splits to
give birth to a pearl

out of its womb.
The half bloomed star
gets menstruated.
The bud in the garden
gets impregnated.

A blue catastrophe
finds amorous fulfilment
with the flying bee
sucking the nectar form
the flowers.

A few moments of
intimacy
lends to abysmally narrow
dungeons of misfortune
where a little rare
happiness
evaporate
like droplets of water
into thin desert air of
the native earth.

The lap of mother earth with all its
fragmentation
feels the tremor of an
uncanny kind
the loud voice of the
silence
is disseminated
in the quivering sky
undulating sea and
the ever resilient earth.

The Shrien of silence
perturbs none
other than the
God
facing repeated deaths
each moment.

# A Bend in the Equation

Each equation of
Life and
Death
on certain occasions
seems
more certain than
semi-colons.

But a twist
With startling metaphors of uncertainty
and
polished syntax of volatility
make every number and symbol
of algebraic proportions
seems more
undecipherable and
undefinitive.
Each revelation becomes a
fallacy.

Time moves along
its
linear / circular
axis.
Beyond the binaries of
good and

bad
black and
white
at the other end of the
horizon
A misguided pilgrim
and
an abstruse lover
wears the same
enigmatic mark
on the forehead of
anguish.

On the tombstone of
inherited legacy
an invisible figurine
in an angelic voice
narrates the nuanced idioms of
the Path and
Destination
with Destiny
correlating the two.

Movement follows the
Momentum.
Gesture follows the
Intimacy.
Death follows the
Life.
Flowers follow the
impregnated buds.
Lines follow the
Arc.

Petals follow the
Stem.
A bend in the Equation
remains as
residues
in the final end of the
beginning.

# Sunrise in California

Against the vast emptiness of the
Sky
the blurred lines on the landmass
in a cruel beguiling way
divide the globe along native instincts
to keep every chunks
in perpetual servitude.

The unending quest for
'Real darkness and
unreal light
ends / begins
at the shadowy lines
of the corpse.

Out of the dying corpse
in flames
A 'SELF'
Yours,
Mine may be,
erupts
surreptitiously
only
to wither away

in the etherscape
beyond the limits
of the Unknown.

Defying the perimeter of the
the great void
cracking the innermost sanctum
into shards.

The 'Self' with all its
eerie virtues
and
sublime vices
meditates on the graveyard
and
declares
with all stubborn innocence
the singularity
within all fractured 'selves'.

The Sun that rises in
the eastern sky of
India
finds its reflection
in the hinterland of California
with all its inconsolate
radiance
and
desolate luminosity.

# God Soliloquises

One fine morning
sunshine of
Pearls and
sapphire are
seen swinging
on the grasslands and
the sea shore.

Buds blooms into flower
seeds are germinated into
fruits
Butterfly sucks the nectar
The life cycle of fruits
and
seeds
moves,
moves with a greater momentum
to reach the
netherworld where
life succeeds death.

The golden voice of
Paddy field
and
the lyrical poetics of
sea waves

reverberate
our ambience
with rich colors of
vibrancy and
buoyancy .

In the late twilight period of
the day
a noble soul
with the blessings of
Village Deity
calculates the movement of
heavenly bodies
and
prognosticates
the soliloquy of
God.

Time doesn't move in a linear direction.
The stream of life speaks of
certitude of uncertainty.
Man is poor in the midst of
the rich repertoire of Nature.
Man seeks vicarious pleasure
in the outer embellishments
of life.
The Truth of life
escapes
in the fallacious grandeur
of
living.
God soliloquises.

# Multiple Horizons

*To have loved one horizon is insularity; it blind-folds vision. It narrows experience.*
*- Derek Walcott*

My own yard is strewn with
the twinkling stars and
nebulous dust of the
Milky way.

And yours
a moon with
its envious black smudges
soothing light with
Sweet darkness
of
memories.
The stench of darkness
mocks
the eerie radiance.

The road that stretches
from my doorway
leads,
Leads in reversible momentum
and
elongates

elliptically though,
to a corner
where moon waxes and
sun wanes
to the billowing emotions of
mine.

The journey from your
mud house
neatly picks up the
turbulent dark to
flame a million light
blazes the trail of the horizon
at the other end.

In the wee hours of a
blessed morning
the apparent lines of
separation
between you and
me
are getting blurred,
pointing out the flaws of the
Equation of Relationship.

A little while before
the twilight
we,
you and me
are scattered under
the shade of the
branches and branchlets
of a peepul tree.

Talking to one another
we now comprehend the
futility of a mad rush
to touch the
nadir / zenith of the
horizon
lone and
singular.

Multiple horizons co-habit
peacefully
between the blank spaces
you and
me
leave behind.

# The Butterfly flaps its wings

Cracks in the wall
pulsate with psychedelic colors
and
lines against stark white background
tears apart apparently
the elusive intimacies of
yesterday.

Despite all the cacophony
of dispossession
the shadow of intense longing
and love
looms large
on the spatial hinterland of
emigres.

The thirst of future
ends
the hunger of yesterday
set the tone of the song of
journey
where the fractured selves
aspire to be with the
whole.

The verdant valley
of the creative dreams of the
Displaced
is no where seen
hither and
tither.

The chiseler
on this bank of the
Mediterranean sea
knows
the intricacies of
carving a bosom.

He
however
doesn't leave the hammer
and the craftsmanship.

Rather
he waits for the sunshine
from the other shore of the
Atlantic Ocean
where
he can drench himself.

The pregnant sea
gives birth the first ray of
Sunshine
the luminosity of which
is dispersed on the waves
and
the casuarinas

near an oasis of the
desert.

On the sterile branches of the
half-dead tree
a thirsty butterfly
flaps its wings
to set off a
storm of hunger
along the
predictable lines
in the space
that the immigrants claim
to be their own
source of
Life.

# The Downward Branches

With a palmful of
sensuousness
a tree lies asleep
in the sacred lap of my
mother.

Inhaling the
aura and
aroma of the tree
the branches,
undress themselves
caress the delicate organs
of the earth
with accentuated libido.

Unfazed,
a girl in her adolescence
relishes,
quenches her carnal hunger
gets shaken and
ashen
in sensual empathy.

Dotted with rows of
gulmohar trees
the margins of the

mustard field
sketch a landscape of
love and
sensuality
in disproportionate shapes.

Branch of gulmohar tree
is moistened and
drenched
in the flowing stream, nearby
with
chunks of flesh,
spurts of blood
scattered on
the open blue sky.

A fraction of the earth
gets
menstruated
and a tree
is birthed
with branches
embellished on her nude body
To the same womb
the downward branches
return
time and again
in search of roots.

## An Amiable Chaos

We are
the decayed skeletons of
our cherished dreams
a unit, dishevelled
moves unfazed
into the oblivion of
Eternity.

Aflame
the stone of life in
ruins
with the Divine Judgement of
Cosmic curse
we,
in a frenzy of
false enlightenment
pronounce, aloud
in an undeciphered text
the total victory of
the rubbles of the
earth
and
the smoke-filled sky.

In an apparent war of
Life

with earth and sky
what you think to be a
triumphant win
is
in essence
an ascent into the oblivion of
partial defeat
and
total decimation.

A little sense of
obviousness
observes
"The purity of pain is present
in both
victory and
defeat"
The appendage is one with
the multi-layered
original text.

The amphitheatre of
Life
gives everyone a
chance
to perform
the roles assigned
to all
by the
Destiny.

The Curtain is raised
where the

hunter and the
hunted
are in mutual understanding to
create
an amiable chaos
of consonance and
dissonance.

# The Lonely Sailor

Face to face with one's
self
the sailor leaves for the
Deep Sea
knowing fairly well
the depth of the sea
and
the expanse of the ripples.

In twilight
before the sunset
the brimming sea
engagingly
talks to the brilliant white patch
at the edge of the cloud
and
ingratiatingly smiles at the
luminous black spots of the
Moon.

In the pitch dark night
waning moon and
sullen sea
meet
at the point
where

the lonely sailor
oars the boat forward.

In the gleam of moonlight
unknowingly
the sailor moves
in reverse momentum
and
reaches his hut
in the buzzing world of
solitude.

With his unfulfilled desire(s) of
not finding a painted shell
for his daughter
the sailor, almost
religiously
offers a fraction
 of his fulfilling journey
as the last oblation of
Life.

Subtending the arc of the
starry night
the lonely sailor
stalks the shore
with his
solitary shadow.

# An Unfinished Sculpture

Time
gets lost
in the quicksand of
Time itself.
On the broad canvas of
Time
the hands of the Artiste
shivers
as he paints life with
all its hues.

Disarrayed words of a
Poem
seek,
in a futile bid
a space
in the creative orbit of the
Poet.

Giggling darkness
at a distance
steals
the serene violence of the
clouds
and the unquiet murmur of the
grass flowers in the wind.

The image
revealingly
conceals more than the
shadow.

Drifting far away from
the axis of
aesthetics
the sculpture itself
denies
to be sculptured,
apprehending to lose
its soul.

The sculpture remains
half-made and
unfinished.

# The Infidel Time

Behind the Throne of Dust
"I"
with all my possible acquisitiveness
proclaim
the simple banal Truth
that
'I'
Dictate the narrative of
the space within
and
beyond the horizon.
In a word
I
control the movement and
momentum of
Time.

Unknowingly,
lurking faintly within
my memory
the Oracle of Delphi
in a hushed tone
whispers'
'Time is notorious for its
infidelity,
spurns the old, dishevelled

footprints and chases
the new ones
only to be discarded
after some moments.
It erases
everything,
much to my
discomfort and
annoyance.

Unmasking
all the allurements of
my pseudo crafty skills
Time
scratches the bases
and
exposes the innards of my
gullible craftsmanship.

Now
the lyrics of pathos
are coming out of the
empty cisterns and
broken flute.
I
In the final chapter
live the life of
the Dead.

# Immodest Shadow

A tree
in the Elysium
bears only one
forbidden fruit
others are redundant.

A drop of
nectar
from the cup of
hemlock
seeks a
Socratesque unalloyed
Truth.

Down the line of the
Ethereal space
the image strides behind the
shadow
in the golden shine of sunrays
the shadow then
in the evening
rises to defy the
deferential authority of the
Image.

In an irony of sorts
the corn denies
the existence of seed
the child unacknowledges
the identity of the
womb.

The disjointed structure of
Canons
in the state
make the barbarous king
declare
the death of the
Nightingale
on the withered stumps
of the tree.

Lending the ears
to the Sermons on the Mount
the King,
in the long run
upto the Ultimatum
realises
the hard truth
cloaked in soft lies
'The Immodest shadow
can't define
the contents of the Image'
Beauty retains its
Identity
without any adjectival allurements.

The Nightingale begins to
sing
in its inviolate voice.

# Dust Aswirls in Sunshine

A drop of 'selfishness'
and
a tiny particle of 'Ego'
make way for the creation of
God.

Rewriting
the elegy of sweet arrogance
and
bitter innocence
on the walls of the caves of
Aborigines
the Man evokes the motif of
Absurd Divinity.

The sullen twilight
descends on the
rooftop of the
Castle
where
a tedious argument of
insidious intent
ensues,
between
God and
Man.

An overwhelming question
persistently
stares us all
"Can a visible line be drawn
between an image
and
a shadow ?
'How does ethereal luminosity
inspire
the smell of the soil' ?

In the dialogic ambience of
Time
between the two
in quick response to the
Bliss of God
Man
offeres a handful dust
which
aswirles in the sunshine
becomes
a burnished throne of
pearls and
sapphire.

# The Cathartic Pause

In the sterile bonhomie of
Life
everything moves
either
a linear path
or
an orbital axis
upto a point of
Infinity.

The grass sings
in the faint moonlight
The grasshopper jumps over
the tumbled graves
The dragonfly flaps its wings
to hoodwink
the little child
out
to hold it
with his tiny fingers.

In this very
unusual moment
there lies
no hermit
under the shade of the

peepul tree
in search of
salvation.

Each one of us
is
a half-finished
athlete
in the calendered track of
living.

Each one of us
is
in the cocoon of
self-denial
to seek the routes of
expediency.

A poet hardly looks at the torn papers
from the dustbin
in search of a
half-blossomed alphabet.

An artist
seldom cares for
the spilt color
which bears
the bud of
a gulmohar tree.

In the arena of
immediate prudence
He

is lured into the
blind alley of
quantified acquisition
losing the courage of surrendering
to a moment of
Eternity.

Man
seeks a breathing space of
Cathartic Pause
in the Ultimate Equation of
Life.

# Ashore comes the Oarsman

The Deep Sea doesn't forget
the sand dunes of the Shore.
The mighty masculine
sea-waves
every now and then
visit the
feminine shore
with gifts of pears and
painted sea-shells.

The barges drift
with the turning tide
each time.
The imprint of the roaring waves
gets obliterated
each moment.

In the frosty silence of the
morning
the Oarsman
moves to the sea
in his torn-tarred boat
to explore
the territory of
El Dorado
where

maximum pleasure is bought
with minimal efforts.

Market yard, there
is peopled with neuter genders
to choose,
in a futile bid
their chieftain.
The thunder of spring is
heard
from the distant mountains.

At a point
where
the ambience doesn't recognise
the character
in its immediate circumference
the oarsman questions himself
of his
existential relevance
in the Grand Design of
Time.

Humbly numbed and
dejected
he comes out of the
cesspool of
possessive stupor
and
turns the wheel
with a windward glance
towards the shore
in real quest of the

rockpebbles.
counting his
sick mother,
broken hut
skeletal residues of
his Destiny
and, moreover
a fraction of
himself.

# Fall of the Last Petal

The last petal of the flower
falls
to touch the ground
and
loses its existence.

Contrary to the amorous look of the
butterflies, around
the apparently torn petal is
overjoyed
to find its another death.

Out of the glowing embers
and
smoldering fire
the petal takes a
rebirth
from the womb of the
menstruated Mother Earth.

The ever-renewing cycle
of
Transformation and
obliteration
is
perpetually impregnated
with

a vast array of
unsprouted seeds.

Down the stream of
Time
the narratives of futurity
flow
into the oceans of past.

The differentiated categories
of all hues
along the passage of Life
get diminished,
blurred ultimately
to proclaim
the axiomatic Truth.

"Life,
The ever present,
knows no finality,
no finished crystallisation".

The flower
and
its petals
are there
where,
its has been
from the beginning
without any
smudges of
tender touch.

*The Beast has a bear's body, a lion's mane, a buffalo's head, a boar's tusks and a wolf's tail and legs. The Beast becomes a human after the last petal falls from the rose.*

**Black Eagle Books**

www.blackeaglebooks.org
info@blackeaglebooks.org

Black Eagle Books, an independent publisher, was founded as a nonprofit organization in April, 2019. It is our mission to connect and engage the Indian diaspora and the world at large with the best of works of world literature published on a collaborative platform, with special emphasis on foregrounding Contemporary Classics and New Writing.

www.ingramcontent.com/pod-product-compliance
Lightning Source LLC
Chambersburg PA
CBHW060617080526
44585CB00013B/876